The Science of Reptiles

LIVING SCIENCE

Janice Parker

Gareth Stevens Publishing
A WORLD ALMANAC EDUCATION GROUP COMPANY

For a free color catalog describing Gareth Stevens' list of high-quality books and multimedia programs, call 1-800-542-2595 (USA) or 1-800-461-9120 (Canada). Gareth Stevens Publishing's Fax: (414) 225-0377.

Library of Congress Cataloging-in-Publication Data

Parker, Janice.
    The science of reptiles / by Janice Parker.
        p. cm. — (Living science)
    Includes index.
    Summary: An illustrated introduction to the physical characteristics, habits, and natural
environment of various members of the reptile family.
    ISBN 0-8368-2681-7 (lib. bdg.)
    1. Reptiles—Juvenile literature. [1. Reptiles.] I. Title. II. Living Science (Milwaukee, Wis.)
QL644.2 .P36 2000
597.9—dc21   00-028527

This edition first published in 2000 by
Gareth Stevens Publishing
A World Almanac Education Group Company
1555 North RiverCenter Drive, Suite 201
Milwaukee, WI 53212 USA

Project Co-ordinator: Rennay Craats
Series Editor: Celeste Peters
Copy Editor: Heather Kissock
Design: Warren Clark
Cover Design: Lucinda Cage, Terry Paulhus
Layout: Lucinda Cage
Gareth Stevens Editor: Patricia Lantier-Sampon

Every reasonable effort has been made to trace ownership and to obtain permission to reprint
copyright material. The publishers would be pleased to have any errors or omissions brought
to their attention so that they may be corrected in subsequent printings.

Photograph Credits:
Corbis: cover (center). Corel Corporation: pages 4 top, 4 bottom, 6 bottom, 8, 9 top, 9 bottom,
11, 12 left, 12 middle, 13 top, 13 bottom left, 16 left, 17 left, 21 left, 22 top, 22 bottom, 23 bottom,
24 top, 24 bottom, 26, 27 top, 27 left, 27 middle, 27 right, 27 bottom, 28 right, 29 top, 29 bottom,
31. Brian Keating: pages 14, 15. PhotoDisc: cover (background). Tom Stack & Associates: pages 5
bottom (Joe McDonald), 7 right (Ann Duncan), 10 top (Thomas Kitchin), 10 bottom
(Joe McDonald), 13 bottom right (Tom & Therisa Stack), 17 right (Inga Spence), 28 left
(Joe McDonald), 30 (Tom Stack). Dr. Zoltan Takacs: page 25 top. Visuals Unlimited: pages 5 top
(Tom J. Ulrich), 6 top (Rick Poley), 6 left (G. Perkins), 7 left (Jim Merli), 12 right (Tom J. Ulrich),
16 right (Cheryl A. Ertelt), 18 (Hal Beral), 20 (Ken Lucas), 21 bottom right (Tom J. Ulrich), 23 top
(Jim Merli), 25 bottom (Gary Meszaros).

Printed in Canada

1 2 3 4 5 6 7 8 9 04 03 02 01 00

Contents

What Do You Know about Reptiles?

Most people have seen reptiles on television or in zoos. Reptiles are a group of animals with similar features. These features make reptiles different from other animals, such as fish, birds, and insects.

Most reptiles have scaly skin. Turtles are some of the few reptiles that have shells.

Reptile young are usually born on land from eggs. The babies look like small versions of their parents. Reptiles are cold-blooded animals with tough, dry skin. Like birds and mammals, reptiles are **vertebrates**. They have backbones.

We divide reptiles into four main groups. These groups include:
- crocodilians
- lizards and snakes
- tuataras
- turtles

Tuataras are found only in New Zealand.

Crocodiles live in many parts of the world.

Puzzler

Which relatives of reptiles are now **extinct**?

Answer: Many dinosaurs were closely related to the reptiles that live today.

Life Cycles

R eptiles, like all other living things, have a life cycle. A life cycle includes being born, growing, **reproducing**, and dying.

Adult female alligators lay between twenty and sixty eggs at a time. A baby alligator looks like a tiny version of an adult alligator. It keeps growing its entire life but does not change shape. Alligators can live to be sixty years old.

Some reptiles hatch from eggs. Others are born live from their mother's body. The shell of a reptile egg can be soft and leathery or hard like a bird egg.

Most reptile parents do not stay with their eggs. The **hatchlings** must survive on their own. A few reptiles, such as crocodiles, protect the eggs and the young until they can look after themselves.

Young reptiles usually grow slowly. Once they become adult size, they change very little. Many reptiles continue to grow slowly all their lives.

Boa constrictor eggs hatch inside the mother. The newborn snakes are 14–22 inches (36–56 centimeters) long.

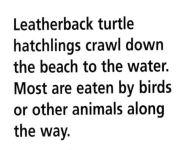

Leatherback turtle hatchlings crawl down the beach to the water. Most are eaten by birds or other animals along the way.

Cold-Blooded Creatures

Reptiles are cold-blooded animals, or **ectotherms**. This does not mean their blood is cold. It means they cannot produce any body heat.

All mammals, including dogs, cats, and people, are warm-blooded animals, or **endotherms**. They produce heat in their own bodies to keep warm.

Lizards cannot control their body temperature. To warm up, they sun themselves on rocks.

Ectotherms change temperature with their surroundings. If the weather is cold, reptiles lie out in the sunshine to warm up. If it is too hot, reptiles move to a cooler, shadier area.

Reptiles must be warm to move quickly so they can hunt and avoid being hunted. When the weather is cool, they cool down and become less active.

Some reptiles change their body temperature by changing their skin color. Darker skin draws in more heat than does lighter skin.

Activity

Finding Ectotherms

Go to a park or wilderness area on a sunny day. Can you find any reptiles basking in the sunshine? Remember to look at sunny areas in trees and on top of rocks.

Tough Skins

All reptiles have dry **scales** or **scutes** covering their bodies. Scales are made of hard material like fingernails. They act like a suit of armor. Scales help protect animals from the environment and from other animals.

Many reptiles, particularly snakes and lizards, shed their top layer of scales as they grow. This is called **molting**. A new layer of scales grows under the old layer before the animal sheds.

Most lizards shed small pieces of skin at a time. It takes the animals a few days to molt.

Snakes usually shed their entire skin at once. This takes about thirty minutes.

Scutes are harder than scales. Turtles and crocodiles have bony scutes on their backs. Scutes do not molt, but they often fall off the animal's body.

Scutes make up the outer layer of many turtles. Soft-shelled turtles have an outer layer that is more like tough skin than bony scutes.

Puzzler

How do scutes help tell the age of an animal?

Answer:
Like tree rings, reptiles add a layer to their scutes each year. Counting the layers helps people guess an animal's age. Scutes do wear off, so this method is not exact.

Reptile Types

Nearly eight thousand types of reptiles roam the world today. These are divided into four main groups. Other reptiles are extinct. They are no longer around.

Types of Reptiles

Crocodilians

- hatch from eggs
- have scutes
- live in or near water
- 23 types

Lizards and Snakes

- have scales
- most hatch from eggs, some born live
- tongues sense smell
- 7,545 types

Tuataras

- hatch from eggs
- have a third eye
- spikes run down back and tail
- 2 types

Examples

alligators, caimans, crocodiles

cobras, iguanas, rattlesnakes

both types called tuatara

Reticulated pythons wrap themselves around prey and squeeze it to death.

Turtles

- hatch from eggs
- live longer than other reptiles
- shell of scutes protects body
- 292 types

Extinct Reptiles

- dinosaurs
- ichthyosaurs–ancient swimming reptiles
- pterosaurs–ancient flying reptiles

box turtles, Galápagos tortoises, sea turtles

Elasmosaurus, Pteranodon, Tyrannosaurus rex

Working with Reptiles

Some people are so interested in reptiles, they decide to work with them. **Herpetologists** are people who study reptiles and amphibians. Most have at least one degree in science from a university or college. Some herpetologists work to protect reptiles that are **endangered**.

Herpetologists study snakes, lizards, and other reptiles. What they learn about reptiles is useful to people working in other sciences, such as ecology and biology.

Many **veterinarians** and veterinary assistants also work with reptiles. These medical workers help make sure that pets, including reptiles, stay healthy.

Zookeepers care for reptiles that live in zoos. They feed the animals and clean out the areas where they live. Sometimes zookeepers help breed reptiles.

Zookeepers often work with veterinarians to nurse reptiles' wounds and to make sure the animals remain healthy.

Activity

Do Your Own Research
Many people have jobs that involve reptiles. Have a parent or teacher help you discover more about these careers:

- herpetologist
- pet shop worker
- veterinarian
- zookeeper

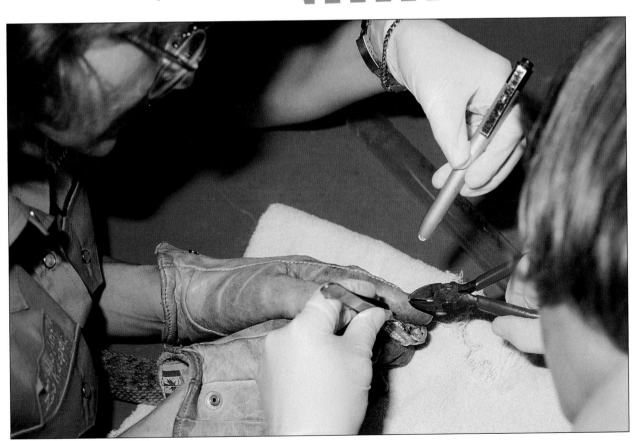

Crocodilians

There are four types of crocodilians: alligators; caimans; crocodiles; and gavials, or gharials. Crocodilians spend all of their lives in or near water. These reptiles look much like their ancestors did 65 million years ago.

Types of Crocodilians

Alligators	Caimans

Alligators	Caimans
• grow to between 9 and 12 feet (2.7 and 3.7 m) long	• grow to be around 6 feet (1.8 m) long
• have rounded snouts	• have rounded snouts
• live in China and North America	• live in Central America and South America
• no teeth showing when mouth is closed	• no teeth showing when mouth is closed

Crocodilians move very quickly to attack their prey. Their jaws are lined with teeth. Crocodilians eat mostly other animals. Large crocodilians sometimes catch and eat large mammals, such as horses. Some eat insects and frogs. Others eat fish and birds.

Activity

Categorize Crocodilians

Find photographs of several crocodilians. Decide if each animal is an alligator, caiman, crocodile, or gavial. Hint: Look at the teeth and snout.

Crocodiles

- grow between 8 and 23 feet (2.4 and 7 m) long

- have long, pointed snouts

- live in North America, South America, Africa, Australia, and India

- fourth tooth in lower jaw shows when mouth is closed

Gavials

- grow to around 20 feet (6 m) long

- have long, skinny snouts

- live in India and Nepal

- all teeth show when mouth is closed

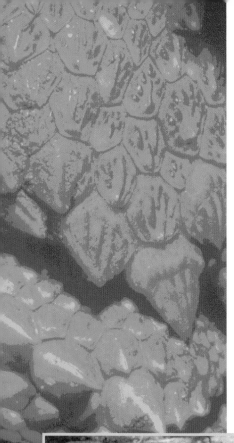

Lizards and Snakes

Lizards come in all shapes and colors. The tails of most lizards are longer than their bodies. Many lizards can lose their tails to get away from **predators**. The tails later grow back. Some lizards have no legs at all and look like snakes.

Some snakes can grow to be very long. The anaconda can grow to be more than 25 feet (8 meters) in length. The thread snake, on the other hand, is only about 4 inches (10.2 cm) long.

The largest lizard, the Komodo dragon, can grow to be 10 feet (3 m) long.

All snakes are **carnivores**. They eat other animals. Snakes swallow their food whole. A snake's jaw can separate, allowing it to open its mouth very wide. Some snakes kill their prey by biting. Others squeeze their prey to death. Both snakes and lizards use their tongues to smell and find prey. Most lizards are also carnivores, but some, such as iguanas and skinks, eat plants.

Types of Snake Movement

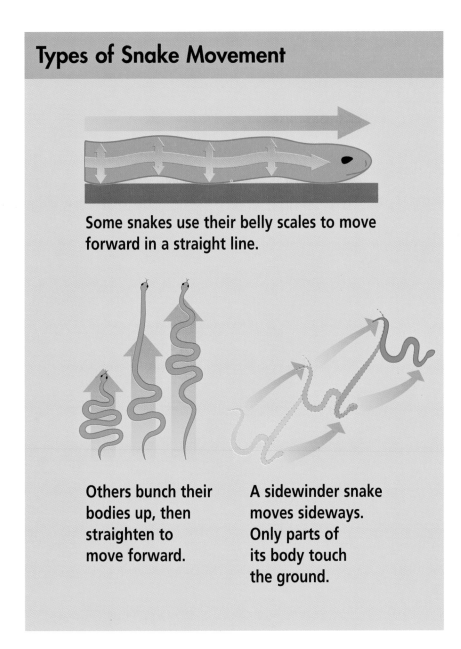

Some snakes use their belly scales to move forward in a straight line.

Others bunch their bodies up, then straighten to move forward.

A sidewinder snake moves sideways. Only parts of its body touch the ground.

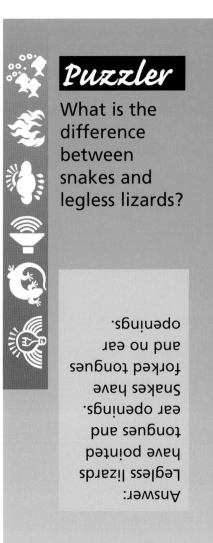

Puzzler

What is the difference between snakes and legless lizards?

Answer: Legless lizards have pointed tongues and ear openings. Snakes have forked tongues and no ear openings.

Tuataras

The tuatara is a lizard-like animal that has a row of spikes down its back and tail. A few features make it different from a lizard. The tuatara's skull has a different shape than a lizard's skull. The tuatara also has a third "eye" on its forehead. This eye is very sensitive to light and dark. When the tuatara is six months old, the eye becomes covered by a scale.

Tuataras eat insects, other small animals, and bird eggs. They grow up to 28 inches (71 cm) in length and can live to be one hundred years old.

Tuataras are nocturnal. They sleep all day and hunt at night.

Tuataras are living **fossils**. Animals almost exactly like tuataras lived on Earth nearly 200 million years ago. Tuataras can show us how those ancient reptiles lived. Today, tuataras are found only on a few islands near New Zealand.

Many of New Zealand's wild animals were brought there from other countries. The tuatara, however, is native to the area.

Puzzler

How did the tuatara get its name?

Answer:
The Maori people of New Zealand named it for the spikes down its back. Tuatara means "peaks on the back" or "lightning back" in Maori.

Turtles, Tortoises, and Terrapins

Achelonian (ki-LOH-nee-un) is a reptile that has a shell. Chelonians live in many different **habitats**. They can be found in oceans, lakes, forests, and deserts. Chelonians include turtles, tortoises, and terrapins.

A shell helps protect chelonians from the environment and predators. It is made of two parts. The upper part is the **carapace**. The part underneath is the **plastron**. These two parts join at the side of the reptile's body.

The shell of a sea turtle is flatter than the shell of a land tortoise. A flat shape helps the turtle move through water quickly.

Hatchlings need to dig out of their eggs, find food, and stay safe from predators, all without help from their parents.

Activity

Reptile Research
What is the difference between turtles, tortoises, and terrapins? To find out, use library books or a few of the web sites listed at the back of this book.

Some chelonians lay more than one hundred eggs at a time. Other animals like to eat young chelonians. Few hatchlings survive for more than a couple of years. Those that do survive can live for a very long time. For example, a Galápagos tortoise can live for more than 150 years.

The Galápagos tortoise is one of the largest tortoises in the world. It can grow to be 4 feet (1.2 m) long.

Reptile Homes

Reptiles live in many different habitats. They can be found on every continent except Antarctica. Some reptiles even survive in the Arctic! Most reptiles live in warm climates. They live on the ground, in trees, in the sea, or underground.

Most sea snakes live in the warm areas of the Indian and Pacific Oceans.

Snakes can live in deserts, forests, oceans, trees, and under the ground. Islands rarely have snakes.

Reptiles have features that help them survive in their habitat. For example, the emerald tree boa's green color helps it disappear in the rain forest. The tree boa's body is also round on top and flatter on the bottom. This shape keeps it from slipping off tree branches.

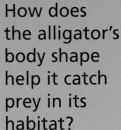

Puzzler

How does the alligator's body shape help it catch prey in its habitat?

Answer:
An alligator's eyes and nostrils sit high on its head. They remain above water as the alligator sits under the water. When the prey gets close enough, the alligator pounces on it.

The Tokay gecko lives in trees and on cliffs. Small threads on the end of its toe pads allow it to climb and hang upside down.

Long bodies and hard, strong heads help worm lizards burrow through the ground.

Web of Life

The web of life shows how all living creatures are connected. Every living thing has its own important role in nature. A food chain shows how animals survive by eating plants or other animals. Energy passes from one living thing to another in a food chain. A food web connects food chains.

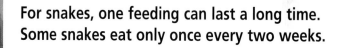

For snakes, one feeding can last a long time. Some snakes eat only once every two weeks.

Reptiles play a significant role in the environment. Many reptiles eat insects. Without these reptiles, there would be too many insects in the world. Other reptiles are a source of food for larger animals.

Activity

Chart a Food Web
Choose a reptile. Find out what it eats and what animals eat it. Draw a food web for your reptile.

Food Web

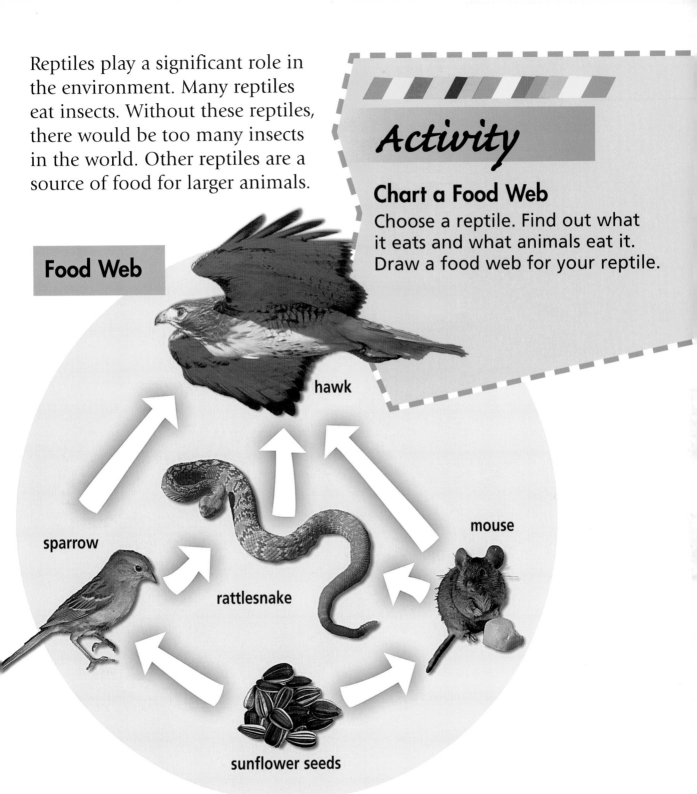

hawk

sparrow

rattlesnake

mouse

sunflower seeds

A snake food web begins with plants and seeds. Small mammals and birds eat the plants and seeds. Some of these animals are then food for snakes. Some snakes may also eat fish and birds. Snakes are food for other animals, especially hawks and owls.

See Ya Later, Alligator

Many reptiles have special ways of protecting themselves from being eaten. **Camouflaged** reptiles, for example, are the same color and pattern as the area in which they live. Reptiles that live in trees are often green in color. Those that live on the ground are often a muddy brown. They are difficult to see if they remain still.

Mimicry
makes harmless snakes look like dangerous snakes. The corn snake looks like the albino coral snake. Predators think the corn snake is poisonous, too.

Playing Dead
protects some snakes when predators approach. The hognose snake lies on its back with its mouth open. Animals that like to eat live food leave the snake alone.

Spiky Scutes

protect many reptiles from being eaten.
Other animals do not want to be pricked by
the scutes. They stay away.

Puzzler

How does
the regal
horned lizard
frighten away
its predators?

Answer:
This unusual
lizard shoots
its own blood
at other
animals to
keep them
away.

Changing Color

hides the chameleon.
Its skin color changes
with the light level,
temperature,
and mood of
the animal.

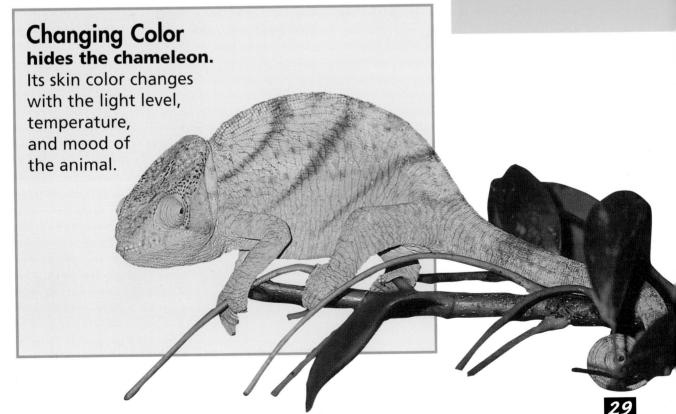

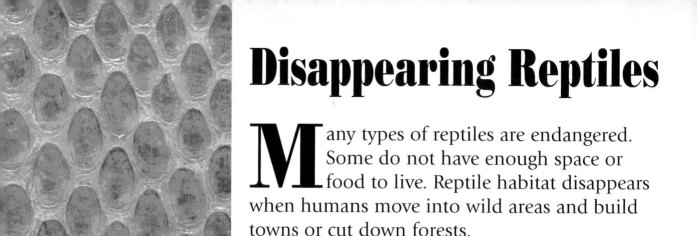

Disappearing Reptiles

Many types of reptiles are endangered. Some do not have enough space or food to live. Reptile habitat disappears when humans move into wild areas and build towns or cut down forests.

Other reptiles are overhunted. Humans kill reptiles for their skin, bones, and meat. Many countries have special laws to protect reptiles and other endangered animals.

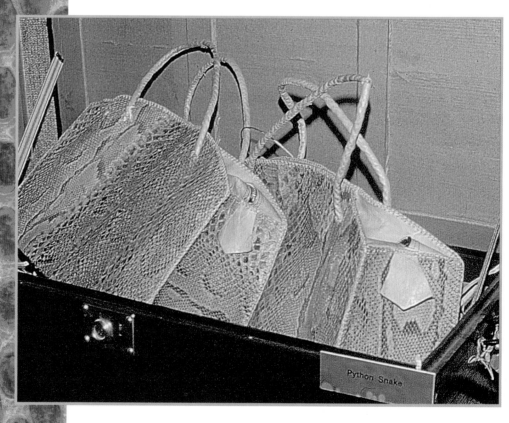

Python Snake

Some reptiles are killed for their beautifully colored skins. The skins are made into souvenirs, clothing, and luggage.

There are many things you can do to help protect endangered reptiles. Here are a few:

1. Reptile skin is often used to make boots, purses, jackets, or belts. Do not buy clothing that is made from the skin of an endangered reptile.
2. If you buy a pet reptile, make sure it was raised in captivity. Pet stores should not take reptiles from a wild environment.
3. Keep natural areas clean. Garbage left on the ground can be dangerous to animals. Pollution can damage an animal's habitat.
4. Learn more about endangered reptiles in your area. Write to a local university or zoo. See if there is anything you can do to help save an endangered animal.

Hawksbill turtles are the sole source of authentic "tortoise shell." They are hunted for their shells and for food even though their meat can be poisonous.

Glossary

camouflage: a disguise that helps plants and animals disappear into their surroundings.

carapace: the upper part of a turtle's shell.

carnivore: an animal that eats other animals.

chelonian: a reptile with a shell.

ectotherm: an animal whose body temperature changes as its environment heats or cools.

endangered: in danger of becoming extinct.

endotherms: animals that produce heat in their bodies to stay warm.

extinct: no longer living anywhere on Earth.

fossil: the stony remains of a plant or animal that lived long ago.

habitat: the place in which an animal naturally lives.

hatchlings: baby animals that have just come out of their egg shells.

herpetologist: a person who studies reptiles and amphibians.

molting: shedding the outer layer of skin or fur.

nocturnal: being active at night.

plastron: the bottom part of a turtle's shell.

predators: animals that hunt other animals for food.

reproducing: making offspring.

scales: tough, waterproof plates that cover the bodies of some reptiles, such as snakes and lizards.

scutes: bony plates that cover the bodies of some reptiles, such as turtles and crocodiles.

vertebrates: animals that have a backbone.

veterinarian: an animal doctor.

Index

Web Sites

www.lazoo.org/reptiles.htm

www.dinosaurvalley.com/kidzone.html

www.worldkids.net/critters/reptiles/welcome.htm

www.turtles.org/kids.htm

Some web sites stay current longer than others. For further web sites, use your search engines to locate the following topics: *alligators, crocodiles, lizards, reptiles, snakes, tuataras,* and *turtles.*